NEVER MORE THERE

NEVER MORE THERE

Stephen Rowe

Nightwood Editions

Gibsons, BC | 2009

Nightwood Editions
P.O. Box 1779
Gibsons, BC VON 1V0
Canada
www.nightwoodeditions.com

COVER DESIGN & TYPESETTING
Carleton Wilson

Tree images, used with permission of Dr. Reese Halter, from *Native Trees of British Columbia*, by Dr. Reese Halter and Nancy J. Turner, Global Forest Science: www.globalforestscience.org.

Nightwood Editions acknowledges financial support from the Government of Canada through the Book Publishing Industry Development Program and the Canada Council for the Arts, and from the Province of British Columbia through the British Columbia Arts Council and the Book Publisher's Tax Credit.

Printed and bound in Canada

LIBRARY AND ARCHIVES CANADA CATALOGUING IN PUBLICATION

Rowe, Stephen, 1980–
    Never more there / Stephen Rowe.

Poems.
ISBN 978-0-88971-239-3

    I. Title.

PS8635.O8855N47 2009   C811'.6   C2009-903157-4

Contents

I.

II.

III.

To my family, past and present.

I

Transient

From the TCH Gander Lake
is alive, pulls itself along, slinks in
on horizon, its stomach flat to earth.
The wind (cooler in this part of the province)
brings whitecaps to water, a shield
to miniscule eco-shifts:
chilled climate, migratory birds,
leaves falling brown (O the little
autumnal losses!), intruders
out skirting habitats.
The tightening of skin one feels
in a place like this, stranger,
makes your hair stand on end.

WIND HAIBUN

She's at it again. The stalking. Waiting till you and sleep are about to reconcile that on-again-off-again love. She sweeps scythe feet through the grass out back, tramples flowerbeds, reckless heels kicking wildly. Knocks clapboard with flutters of taut knuckles, flicks the plastic flap on the dryer vent near the door. She's even shaking the apple tree near the window, yelling profanities through the stutter of leaves. It's her: you know that accent, blasts of edged language knifing air.

under covers
skin on skin
   slit eye moon

I stopped to ask directions. Courteous, he thought awhile, then said, "Too many intersecting roads. It's easy to get lost. Best to take that old horse as far as he'll go. He knows the road. When he stops, get off, and he'll come back alone."

– Matsuo Bashō, *The Narrow Road to the Interior* (Tr. Sam Hamill)

your name is my name

our name is bones

– Fred Wah, *Waiting For Saskatchewan*

1

You in Scotland during the war, part of the Forestry Unit. Black work boots, hat, shirt and suspenders gripping trousers. You're bent over, legs solid as spruce trunks, holding a shovel in your large hands. A man is sitting on the scoop, hoisted above ground, feet dangling, mouth wide with amazement.

greyscale image
tattered edge
    crease through your face

2

On a cargo ship off Australia you watch the sand-coloured horizon line. The sky above is deep blue; below the water appears slate, mixing olive. Lean on the white crusted rail.

whitecaps
crash the hull
    men cheer

in a ring for two deckhands, wrists wrapped in rag bands. Their sweaty arms glisten at dusk. Someone halts the fight. The loser slumps outside the ring, a towel tossed over his shoulder, temple spotted with blood. The winner spits on the deck: *local champion, reputation*. He calls for competition, saliva flicking from fat lips.

sinewy arms
held above shoulders
    the sky

For a time you observe the manner of bouts, shuffles and strikes, how the sailors cry with every jab, how yells crest with fighters' skipping toes, a choral sound. You've stayed away, now say you won't box but will wrestle. A consensus of shouts seals the match.

You're short, but broad in the shoulders; hunched over baring teeth, growling like a Kodiak. You lock arms. The twists of body, torque of form and movement wrenches joints. In the flailing of limbs, cuffing swipes, you pin the boxer to the deck.

above the crowd
the captain waves
    men scatter

salt wind gusts
past the rail
    grappler's breath

3

Sunday evening. A kerosene lamp keeps the room dim. You angle your back against the counter, sleeves rolled up halfway, foot tapping, face vacant. You're singing "The July Drive" like you wrote it, though you heard it in the lumber woods sung by a young man from Kilbride who chewed tobacco, had a flutter in his voice when he told you he lost a brother in France.

Your brother Melvin sits to the table, stares at the floor, clinking a drink of Old Sam. Dad, just a boy, is in the doorway, an elbow overhead propped against the frame, tapping knuckles. Nan smiles and is beautiful in her skin: smooth and fleshy, first wrinkle years away; lifts a damper from the stove, prods splits with a poker. They listen; you sing, your mind working somewhere away from the kitchen heat.

young man spits
in a tobacco tin
   fire crackles

4

Past the Fisherman's Hall with a swagger: you and your brothers into
it again. Uncle San shaking his head, listens at the window to some-
one bawling about a wrecked fence and vegetable garden; downing
the last drop of tea, he plods out the door. Aunt Polly at the scrub-
bing board with shirts and a pair of pants stained with grass, dirt.

cracked palings
broken arm
   Sandy's Bears

5

No breeze passing through the fen today: low lying vegetation, pitcher plants red or purple, juniper twist on their sides, drawn to earth. Mud-clots moist as quicksand in tangles of reed and shrub appear to suck the world inside itself. While dragonflies mate, click their wings between blue-green branches,

a hidden stream
still wild-grass
    trickles

along the half hour walk back to town where houses lean in on themselves, on each other, shouldered roofs. Dependency of structure: *You are where you're from.*

While still a young man you boarded a boat for Halifax, travelled to Singapore, Canberra, Brazil. Five years, no family, no place. Came back, married and worked odd jobs: carpenter, lumberjack, and fisherman: a scant living.

I haven't been able to leave: walking through the fen

boot stuck
in clammy mud
    water rushes by

6

Pieces of you have been elided, handed to me to decode, break down and reconstruct. Never enough and I hate to fill in the blanks around your name. Odysseus has his myths: sirens... sheep's bellies... milk and blood in the sand... Penelope knitting. Three thousand years of story, cracks fleshed-out with caulking. But you're abridged. Strange snippets of legacy that don't fit, like the man you struck on a Singapore dock and left for dead...

the house Max built
washes away
    bridge work

7

Dad. The vowel almost shouts affection. *Pop*. More reverence and awe.

dad|pop   pop|dad   pap|dod   dod|pap

What does one call their father? *Dad*. Grandfather? *Pop*. Great-grandfather? *Pop* or *Great-grandfather*. Great-great-grandfather? *Great-great-grandfather*. *Ancestors*.

You?

Father's father?

scrawl of titles
on yellow paper
    nameless

Spent all morning going through the house to find photos of you (there are three). Dad always hid them to keep them safe, I suppose. In the old house (before the fire) he hung a large portrait of you in the hall. *Beautiful* he said. For years after, each night he'd unplug the appliances, anything with an electrical cord, frayed or not. Mom would go to bed early, shake her head as he fumbled at the outlets.

She had copies made of the other pictures when Dad died; had them restored and hidden in her bedroom dresser, to keep them safe. This is where I find them now, between discoloured pages of the family bible,

grandfather's photos
one more thing to connect
   Mom and Dad

9

Stars freckle the dark after a long day in the lumber woods. It's late, the light's on and three young men are smoking at the table. You roll over, grunt from the top bunk. It's not like you're asking for a long hibernation, just a night of silent sleep.

They've been warned but won't go to bed. The loud one lights a pipe, one more spark in the night's constellation. You toss the covers, drop to the floor, throw yourself forward onto hands solid as a grizzly's. With your heels snatch the pipe from his mouth, fling it at the wall.

cubs scurry to bed
in the quiet dark
    Ursa Major sleeps

Down the harbour, Rowe's Bank just before the tin shop. In a field by the road a man is guiding a plough blade through earth: the slow yielding of grass and soil, metal scraping rock. You're hunched over ahead of him, tackled, leather strapped around shoulders; forehead speckling with sweat, grey shirt sticking to your back. While you finish the work

by a ringle rod fence
cool grass
    the old horse rests

This is memory by proxy. Years ago someone swearing it was the truth told my father. For all the times he recited it to me, the other man remains nameless, forgotten. I'm not even sure it's the right field: near Regular's, now with a tall grass covering. I still remember Dad each time he told the story

eyes wide
staring down the harbour
    I can't see

These Sundays in February: I'm reading Fred Wah who talks about a black bear and remembers his father. Once you climbed a spruce, clung to bark while a bear pawed the trunk, nudged it, tearing at knots, needles, purple cones. Unharmed, you were lucky to see it grunt away an hour later.

yellow sun
between branches
    chewing frankum

What if, ambitious, the bear climbed just high enough to reach your leg? Claws on flesh. The blood runs down the shin, droplets fall from your boot. An exhibition of bone. Carnal relationship, the physicality and presence; not a story remembered after the telling, but body and body in knowing.

I put the book aside and open the window, let winter in. The sudden

rush of white
in a dark room
    eyes awaken

This morning: bears and jealousy.

Nearing fifty your legs weakened. You found it hard to get about or work; had to go on welfare. Chores turned to torture and a man from up the harbour cut wood for the family. Dad said you walked on your hands once just to show you still could. He was young then. In his fifties his legs weakened too: he'd walk to the water tank, a hundred feet to the rail that overlooked the bank, every step burning a memory of you in the doorway watching someone else pile logs

by the shed
an axe on the cutting block
   fists tight

Now at twenty-five my knees give me trouble.

13

Dad was seventeen when he left for Stephenville, just out of high school, handpicked by the bank. Worked long hours, sent money home to you and Nan. The circulation of blood to your legs got worse, slowing you down. Nan became a mother all over again. In the fall Dad came home for the funeral, made the arrangements: chose a casket and pallbearers, approached speakers for the service so Nan wouldn't have to. Went back to the West Coast a week later.

While in university I came home to Heart's Content for Dad's funeral. I remember the leaves seemed as though they couldn't stop falling, wandering the roads, aimless in the wind. We waked him in the church. I stayed with Mom for ten days, chose a casket and pallbearers. While the minister spoke poetry of my father I thought of you lying in bed, a cloth on your forehead, face clammy and pale.

white gloves
leaving the church
   ahead of Nan
      the weight in
      my fingers

14

All this is to say

letters and names on the page. The paper has texture; the sheet of it
levels the playing field. Its edges like barbed wire.

That is to say

let these letters and names be our bones, arrange them here.

That is to say

you'll find me
below the spruce
    a bear rooting soil

TAKING TEA

The morning comes as it always has
    measured steps in a crowded room
    shuffling in careful silence   eyes floorward
       It thirsts for lonesomeness

From my apartment window
the Gander sky is never anything but white or grey
    wearing cloudfolds like togas as it
    strolls indifferently above the plebs' world
       our uncertain tripfoot into tomorrow

In the kitchen the kettle whistles   I take my tea
Move to the chesterfield   half-sitting half-lying
Take a sip   place the cup on the end table
over the ring I've worn in the surface
    I never could be bothered by coasters

The cat drones in the only tone he knows
no doubt hungry without thought of stopping
The table covered with dirty dishes begs for clearing
Clothes writhe on the floor   corpses for cleanup
    Thatkidupstairs throws a tantrum
    over something his mother won't give him
    or something he's not allowed to do

Bodies   these shells for desire
It's nice to think there's always more
        I ache from the inside out   watch the world
        how everything wants   the need
        to fill the emptiness where it's felt most

The tea is weak   needs more milk
and just a sprinkle of sugar
        It's not even afternoon and already
I'm out of coffee spoons

I will not describe the light,
                              what it does to the rugs of trees
laid out where deeper earth meets the sea,
where like a seedling I was forced open.
I could not describe it but there it is
inching across the harbour, fingering
grass and lichen and rock,
                              searching
for a memory but less real.
                              I survey the town,
a geographer seeking his bearings: Hogan's Hill,
Beller's Hill, Sunday School Hill,
Station Road, Gunner's Rock, Larry's Path:
each a name from the days of my father and father's father.
Captions loom like the shadow of myself
stretching as dusk comes,
                              making me ever so aware that
I do not know exactly where Gunner's Rock is.
No Hogans have lived in these hushed houses
for as long as I can remember.
                              I will find no train,
no station when I walk the Station Road
last daylight descending banks,
tripping out into the harbour.

                              Is there any wonder
I want to give these places names of my own?
Brand them with moments
like memories, but more real;
walk through this place in sunlight,
                              surefooted,
hands swinging by my sides.

WEAR IT RED AGAINST THE NIGHT

Though the snow has fallen in thick clumps
of winter,
        the world a white litter box,
and winds hiss in another Ice Age,

our cat in all his slothful glory kneads your sweater
like a warm spread of dough.
                Paws sink into
curled fleece, warm folds of red.
                    Nowlan said,

December is thirteen months long, July's
one afternoon:
        words I've seen tossed about,
slammed against the window. Know

that in this place we're a casualty
of air,
    of cold,
        nature's wayward whims:
the way it tosses
           promiscuously
                its love.

Take my skin,
        wear it red against the night:
a sweater, a cat, a hot water bottle
coursing with the little heat a wound can bring.

Some Functions of Calmia

after Don McKay

To grow everywhere. To cling to
aprons of spruce and birch.
To distract the light
in their blossomy white and pink
(the sun crowd-surfing above the moss pit)
so it never meets the earth.
To stare
perfectly still
                while a caribou takes a piss.

To be gooweddy:
the toxin luring goats astray
far from the fence home
you made.
            To be forever in cliques, then
snicker as you wade through their knee-high ghetto, adeptly
hold out the tangle of their hands

to tug at legs, pulling down, down.

II

EARLY SPRING...

stumbles out the door
   a child forced to befriend
   whomever she can

brushes wiry tufts of trees
sticking out and upward
   the season's birch-broom hair

   What's left of snow
      winter's hand-me-down

   stretches to cover
      (partially)
   earth's flabby midriff

She shuffles along
   shoulders high
   fists in pockets

   an eye out for that
      dolled-up bitch around the corner

ON THE TERRA NOVA RAILBED

All around the snow spirits through air,
    the supple flutter of flakes
diving into earth,
an ample buzz in the eardrums.

I take in the dirge of wind,
how it chants the forest polyphonic.
The slight whisper of alders,
                        gravel throat of spruce,
lead me farther down the trail

to the winding aisle I suspect
is an old logging road
long barred,
            spotted with falling shacks,
            skeletons of woodhorses
            that lumber on the stumps of their hooves.

Somewhere beyond the sightline
my grandfather is still felling trees,
knocking the world down with his hands:
    a wild percussion of axe,
    heart jolt,
chopping away at the sunken mudscape:

an exertion heard for miles.

I find myself snapping pictures
of colossal trunks,
                    broken spruce curled and split,
ghosts driving back into the bog,
old man's beard clutching brittle treeskins.

The strange urgency in their voice.
The bone inheritance I've come to know.

The Blacksmith

a hymn of sorts to Hephaistos

I knew him when he lived downhill
from the farm and old lumber mill
where, by Rock Road, he kept his smithy shop.
I'd stop at times to see

how his hammer struck the shining
iron on the anvil, tossing
bright orange stars into the black-smoke air.
He'd glare with every whack

at the twisted metal and mould
he'd hang as horseshoes to be sold.
Gentle, he'd take the hooves between his legs:
sharp pegs, hands warm and lean.

When one summer he met young Grace
the wrinkles rose on his dark face.
He walked straighter, his wardrobe clean and white:
lighter soles I'd not seen.

They went around town together
arm in arm, as if by tether,
but she grew tired of his grey hair and gout,
backed out. In the smoke air

of his shop he'd whistle and pound
the iron, letting the dull sound
echo up the road. Never mentioned her,
though summer came and went.

The Balladeer

The balladeer sings soft and low,
moaning up on the late-night stage
as round and round the dancers go.
The balladeer

has known the love, has known the rage,
has known the footfalls long-drawn slow
each pencilled down on line and page.

The evening drifts on heel and toe
as dancers blow before the stage:
they waltz around, around below
the balladeer.

From Polka to Reel

a hymn of sorts to Pan

Atop a mountain the fire's edge
lights a tangerine face. On a sunken backpack
navy jeans and black jacket
become a camouflage hunched
in midnight's nothing.

His mouth presses a wooden fipple,
fingertips hammer the grooves in a hollow shaft
as he plays to a cheering circle; a dribble
of saliva wells at the open end.

Melody and slapping hands collide in double
jig time; the barrage of boots on stone
and balsam root pounds out the intensity of now.

From polka to reel a pink cheek scar
bulges with intake of charcoal air,
a memory carved into him:

> *at the hunt one morning   bare trees standing*
> *from the frozen soil like hair on the nape*
> *of his neck   he met the cat*

> *shaggy   gravel-grey   with tasselled tufts*
> *of black on its ears   In silence*
> *it sprung from a wrinkled bough and*

clasped his parka   a single talon ploughing
flesh   the damp softness of fur
against his skin and snow-sprinkled beard

He's tongued the whistle-pipe again,
shuffles it between hands in front of the blaze,
enfolded by shouts and laughter. He adjusts his collar
raising shoulders to cover his branding in these hills.

He sits, hoofing earth,
wants the shriek sound;
runs a fingernail along his cheek,
lips wrapping the instrument once more.

MESSINES

On TV this morning I watched a farmer of Messines
who must be near seventy, dressed in earth-bruised overalls,
striped woollen socks to his knees and a waving red kerchief,
react to the news that underneath him thousands of pounds

of active TNT, left from a British attack in the First World War,
still incubates in a subterranean chamber below his house.
Hands in pockets, he took three steps into the Belgian wind
and stomped the shaking grass, the fragile soil

that gave him nearly enough to raise four spindly sons
and keep a wife of forty years, now full of cancer.
How he says it, so sedate, resigned with a slight nod
as one would talking with an old friend: *You get used to it.*

FIELD WORK

a hymn of sorts to Hermes

He pulls the pitchfork from a bale of hay,
its rusty spikes dull to light, grips an iron bucket
rattling between his calloused fingers, saunters out
where early morning leaves him looking tall. We wait

for his cap's worn peak to sink into earth sloping
toward the town; you first and I behind,
emerge from a copse of alders, bolt to the fence,
leap the wooden couplet. Sprint to the barn,

lift the hasp, let the door groan wide.
My sneakers land on scattered stalks of hay, break
the silence. From a rail the cow turns her head,
gawks at me, her lower jaw sliding from side

to side. I think of the snot running along her lips,
is munched with cud; how pink a nose can be;
the size and depth of her eyes: *I will not be the one
to make this place an abattoir. Don't worry girl.*

We kneel inside the stall, giggle as I palm
teats that give way between my fingers.
Teats. I laugh outright. Then a stream of milk
splashes the floor; denim stained with the morning.

You stand and lead the animal into open air.
I follow, slap her haunches, watch her tail
sway as she wades along the fence into the path.
We slip into the trees before the man returns.

SNOW AND SENIORS

This morning the snow's
soaked to its bones in light
        drizzle and won't
be going anywhere.

The bus I'm on revs down
Empire Avenue where the elderly
clear congested driveways.
        I wonder

        why their children don't
give them a breather
or do the work themselves.

As one of the men rests his shovel
        I think of my father:
squint-eyed, dark tan-
gerine cheeks huffing the cold
like car exhaust, his agonized
smile and nicotined teeth.

Up before the rest of us,
a blue tint in the snow,
        his small form contorted
panting shovelfuls into mounds
in front of the house

        to have the job done as if
it were his only.

And this stranger by the road
stands bow-back

the frisson of bicep, of thigh,
heart muscle.

THE HAG

Sallow hands know their way,
fingers follow your skin: hip, abdomen, breast-
bone palmed. The sense of pulse and breath.

Faint moon rays sheath the bed. Fairy-night
falls in cobalt shrouds to wrap about
the waking shaft of you.

Her varicose thighs constrict into a straddle,
tangled tendrils of rabbit wire hair
pitch a tent above your chest.

No perfume, only turbid air.
Lungs take the weight. Hands snuffing you
in the cool of pillow and sheet.

DEATH SONG FOR CROWS

Crows in the slab-grey dawn whipping rain from soused heads,
inking stamps on the margin of sky: you and the trees.

Crows on a green gate, limp shrew in claws, beaks parted
to screak at seagulls, their eyes rolling up from the beach.

Crows with rupturing bursts into air, feathers stinging wind,
beat a way from earth, slap falling pellets of rain.

Crows grown feeble in breath, songs: the symbol made of you
resting near gravestones and the names of the dead.

Crows in the shade of alder limbs, wrick-necked, supine in leaf-bed,
snarled in twine grass, navy plumes twisting with wind.

THE BERRY PICKERS

For nations vague as weed,
For nomads among stones,
Small-statured cross-faced tribes
And cobble-close families
In mill-towns on dark mornings
Life is slow dying.

– Philip Larkin

I see them: hunchbacked
upturned, keel-like
they plod a many-miled harvest,
for nations vague as weed

wade in this rolling berry patch,
pluck fruit from a net
of bushes. They trawl by hand,
for nomads among stones

(these slow shadowed forms)
shun automated pickers.
On this high slope they appear
small-statured, cross-faced. Tribes

of the working hum old songs:
shanties, local ballads
once meant for seaworthy
and cobble-close families.

It stings, aches to face the waves
grown strange with time.
Might as well live
in mill-towns. On dark mornings

they traipse from small houses,
shuffle buckets over earth
for every branch, leaf, berry...
life is slow dying.

GATHERING WOOD

I palm the axe that angles the wall,
stands taunting in stillness
and take it to the woodpile. Start hacking.
Its creature is ravenous, the way it rives

the body with such comfort, such lust,
taking of it a sliver at a time, time
after time: the slabs of bark, the chips
that spring into bluing light, the splits

that want for earth. *There is a life
they're after, the same one you're after.*
Ring by ring chop, then go back in,
arms a basket full of fodder.

TRIOLET FOR A MOTHER

a hymn of sorts to Demeter

Take the day lilies in your palm,
do not mourn their closing when the sun has ridden away.
Think of their petals in a light morning rain: yellow, speckled, calm.

Take the day lilies in your palm
and, when summer tears come, swathe your ring finger with their
    ruffles, hum a psalm
as your daughter does. On this observance of her wedding day

take the day lilies in your palm,
do not mourn their closing when the sun has ridden away.

The river's light bobble,
almost calm.

Where grasses underwater
arc and streak, I'm pulled
downstream.

You ask me whether I'm okay,
this learning I do: to tread water
in a shell my width,
paddling against the grain
to find the order of it.

The miles of river,
bare landscape
streaks to a point in the distance,
hills sneak into sky,
their bow-backs warmed by sun.
Deadwood drifts by
for a beaver wandering the stream.
The wind itself huffs defiance,
its breath a nameless blast
    (I'd thought it easy to feel alone out here).

I struggle to turn, my paddle
gurgling the water behind me,
those V-shaped ripples,
nearly lose my balance.
    You do it all so smoothly,
the rebel way you slice the surface,
quiet fitting into water,
easing into currents
that take you where you need to be.

I Knew a Maid

I knew a maid with seaweed skin
who moved along the shore
at evening when the tide came in.

Through salted wisps of autumn air
she waltzed as on a floor
while brushing sea lice from her hair.

Those tresses flowed like undertows
and shone with winter hoar,
floating from her, high and low.

I followed then without a care,
along the water's roar,
as she brushed sea lice from her hair.

She rested on a wave-worn stone
beside a rotting oar,
the jutting white of broken bone,

and crossed into the vapour where
a groundswell braced the shore,
while brushing sea lice from her hair.

He Skims Water on a Snowmobile

Where frozen earth ends he
bursts into being   creates
his own wind   tumbling funnel of air
The cold as energy   primordial fuel
propelling him beyond sense
A flurry of wind whips
uncovered skin   he's caught
in the faceripping fury of now

        Treads below
make an usher of ice
that which bears him letting go and suddenly
there's no *before*

Spruce   Rock   Hill   Water   Blood

A congregation of the world just waiting
for Kinneret to take him in its deep blue
    clutch his carriage   legs and leggings
unzip the chest and race into lungs
        choke him into sleep

In a moment it's over   The pond slack-jawed
the foaming wake a wound flushed
a scar bared to sky   stuttering scramble
for breath left behind

The rush of climax
the unholy
letdown of survival

A Pre-emptive Dirge of Sorts for My Grandfather

Bakeapple jam, or rather cloudberry,
that mystery you lifted from the jar
swift stroke into air,

           light swipe onto bread
Nan made in the morning. Hot tea
fogging the wrinkles of your face.

Afternoons I played in the mill: saw each log,
dry-barked cracked limbs of forest,
taken from the dark corner

           (your arms thick as cabers)
lined up before the blade, tense in waiting.
I'd try to count the age rings until they vanished
in a swirl of blurred wood chips.

Later I would hear how you'd slipped,
took the saw through your right hand; stood back,
the shaking wrist broken,

           hung by a split of flesh.
Just staring.

After the surgery my mother said she couldn't
understand you, cursed each time
she saw the mill door unhasped and you
laying logs on the plane.

           An utter mystery! Why...?

I wanted never to know.

VISITATION

a hymn of sorts to Asklepios

You thought life fragile and laid its fragments
on the table, sorted like pills, tablets to take
with supper. No faith in fatalism, each day
was an artwork to craft, your eyes Socratic,
seeking every truth behind experience.

In the emergency room you seemed a portrait
of stained glass. I paced the corridor etherized.
Minutes flushed intravenous, counted in drips,
as names blared across speakers. I remember
how air changes in hospital, the smell of latex.

You wore a tag on one wrist, a cotton bandage
around the other: it was then, after the nights
spent sleepless, appointments, support groups,
the drugs and broken glass, you came to occupy
a space beyond brother: intensely mortal.

III

If I Should Die...

give my body to the sea,
stern uncle of the ice-glare,

that some part of me might rock,
soak back to the Avalonian shore

salt-stung, wave-whipped
among the indifferent flap of seaweed.

But not before you burn my flesh,
the flame's tongue lash and vigour,

strip me of form that this soil,
soft and rich, not be scarred
in my honour.

Down to the Quick

*…the pounded sickle of moon hung thin and weathered
in the southern sky.*

– Patrick Lane

Evening and the day's work done.
He washes his thin hands, squeezes
soap from the dispenser near the sink.

A long day in the classroom
praying to God the kids would get it,
that this place has a literary heritage.

The moon stares, squints through
clouds and the window. He thinks
of his father coming home

from the field: hours put in furrowing:
the lengths of lines drawn in earth,
the look on that face when he saw his son

reading "Flower in the Crannied Wall":
eyes skewed as scythes. He'd lumber oxlike
to supper, fingernails still packed with soil.

He turns off the faucet, hands uncomfortably
clean. Earlier he'd pressed his finger
to the page, pointed out a line to a student;

seeing the ivory colour of his nails
shocked him. Sweeping the air before him,
he reaches for clippers from the cabinet,

then the sharp snap of sickle moons falling.

LORDS OF LARGE EXPERIENCE

1

I hear the noise about thy keel;
I hear the bell struck in the night

Things I want to put in a poem: old movies,
black and whites, the kind that have non-stop raindrops
falling straight to asphalt like sparklers; coffee,
    doughnuts we used to

spin in father's car on the high school grounds when
there was nothing else to do; weekends in the
Musquash casting flies with the muck in our boots;
    telephone calls, one

from my father saying you struck a semi
on the way back home from your sister's house. That
night it rained hard, rattling the windows, droplets
    crackling around you.

2

When the blood creeps, and the nerves prick

Hard to get my head in a place that takes this,
makes some sense of it: in a crumbled chassis,
bent in that accordion crash of impact,
    slumping ahead, head

open, lolling lifeless against the broken
dash. Of course I'm filling in details, searching
for the bigger picture, the *why*, the *how* and
    after these years I'm

still there. Pry apart with the jaws of life this
jumbled thought of you at the end of something.
Find myself years later a fracture, my heart
    stopping when yours did.

3

Could we forget the widow'd hour...

Young men always chasing those girls: top-heavy
dirty-blondes in skimpy bikinis washing
cars, or perky boxers who duke it out, their
    chests the attraction.

What about binge drinkers? Fraternities with
schemes for cash and chicks, the required bad fart jokes:
all the things we thought of in school, the future
    mapped in our weekend

movie rentals. Frivolous placed with what I
watch these days: old classics or drawn-out dramas,
characters whose histories shadow them, who
    ache to forget them.

4

On the bald street breaks the blank day.

Nights when we stayed up till the early morning
watching wrestlers, drinking the beer we'd iced, I'd
leave your lit house, tread through the bluing harbour,
    find it so strange how

fresh things look when grappled by sun, that shine of
muscle pinning night to the west horizon,
ending the excitement before the world waked.
    Try though I may I

can't sit through those matches again, just turn them
over in my head, in a gut-wrenched thought of
you and me, our time in that now-dark house gone,
    down for the three count.

5

We have but faith: we cannot know;
* For knowledge is of things we see....*

Lots to see, too: pictures of you and me with
bats and gloves, balls held in the air that almost
flitter off the film, a kinetic thought just
     waiting for Tuesday

and a lawn to play on. A team of hodgepodge
players, each a batter in time who'd drive that
ball wherever, seeking a hit. I see you
     reaching instead for

sky, to catch the future and pocket it, *yours.*
This is all I know in the summer dream, when
all I have are memories, time, and silent
     walks by unused fields.

6

'Tis well; 'tis something…

Scuffing to the funeral home I didn't
know what to expect. Lots of firsts with you and
this was just another: so many people
   nodding like flowers,

ushers for the walk. As I passed, they spoke but
sounded like the wind by the door. I wanted
Auden's poem, his "Funeral Blues," or one from
   Tennyson uttered

in my father's voice, but he couldn't know. I
turned and roses fell from your girlfriend's tired eyes.
As she held me shaking, you lay so still so
   close in your steel bed.

7

The words that are not heard again.

Not a game, but faith is a thing to play with,
something like that. Not what you want to learn when
belted in, night-speeding one forty into
    traffic. You haul out

pass a Grand Am only to find another
racing headlong, lunging its headlight-halo.
Feel my lips part, listen for shouts but they're lost
    far in the darkness.

Faster, hands tight, foot on the pedal, pray us
out of this. Near miss. As you laugh it off, I
stare at you, mouth words into air and wait for
    night to reply....

WAKING

This morning the harbour
                        is different:
light slumps hard on clapboard
reckless with colour and brightness,
                              the weight
almost tangible. Dampness abounds:
the pavement,
                  that darkness around the eyes
before the ritual of makeup;
                                  gaping pothole pores
and the greasy feeling of waking. Spring grass,
yellow, matted
                  is cool with dew
the way pillows can be cool with drool,
and from deep in the bay's nasal cavity
waves snore steady to the shoreline.

For now she is herself,
                        running bare
through dreams of her own devising,
where splayed maples are more
than a case of sleep-tossed hair.

CAN YOU RIDE HORSES THERE?

The brook splash, the wings of a robin through air,
wind as it wraps around your ears, head,
through long auburn hair, how sunlight
skipping on water has a sound all its own
you can not hear.

    The rock you sit on, damp and hard
    sure beats a hospital bed.

As you dangle toenails in the cool wet,
Bowering Park passes you by like a nineteen year old
in a Mustang booming hip hop down the street,
muffled in the distance.

You feel like falling just to know what it is
to hit the ground

    maybe from a window:
the pause it creates, that space
within a coma,

    the world passing by
while a machine breathes for you,
your mind filled with trails, paths, rivers,
palominos and the tempo of hooves,
your hair strained through wind.

Can the unconscious tune in
    to our static?

And suddenly words are so rare,
and he's there in blue sheets and a johnny coat,
in every *i*, every *u*, his name
like the punch of a kick drum:

unconscious, his mind probing
wavelengths for something to clasp,

or something more intimate:

   a steady gait, hooves on gravel.

Driving the 330 from Gander

Say they're only birch trees,
they're only trees. Don't
think of what that means.

– Lorna Crozier

The land has given up, lain down
sulking for miles, refusing to stand
up to the heavy press of snow.
From a distance the shaking flakes
swarm in a smoky locust-swirl.

It's hard to think of smothering:
that loss of air, tightness of throat,
heaving that rises through lungs
halted near the heart. Too near,
the way death struggles, hits home.

Birch trees streak by the roadside:
torn trunks, branches twisting into
sky: bronchus, bronchiole, trachea
filled with growths of snow, bodies
withered, firm in desperation.

I never could figure out why it took
so long for you to tell me. Going
about daily business, slowing down
only to catch a breather as the rotting
swelled from your inside out,

the air becoming dense in the lungs,
taking life a little breath at a time
until silence was sweeter than speech.
Quiet as window-haunting birch,
their names as harsh as yours.

Late Poem for H.

with apologies to Rilke

This moment I press the one I love to my chest
and know her: the moist warmth of cheek,
pulse through delicate neck, breaths
like tips of long grass on my skin.

Alone where the breeze whispers, *He is gone*,
teasing in the frantic night, it's 2 am and you
wrestle with sheets, entangled in a single bed.
Single. How long has it been? And still the cold
finds its way along your shins, thighs,
a rabid animal stroking your skin
a constellation of goosebumps, shoulders tense,
a dull ache behind your ears, throat.

                    He is gone.
His hands will never mingle with the earth,
never know what forms your flesh,
heat of body, the living like mirrors
of steaming water. Do the dead
remember their dying, the sudden wreckage of it?
Do their creatures haunt them, hurt like
phantom limbs severed, ever present?

I blur into sleep, clutch the naked body I hold,
inhale the scent of hair strewn across my mouth.
She's not given thought to the morning,
if it comes at all, its dreams
distant as monuments to old lovers.

For you I know
the night bares no pretense, tells it like it is:
He is gone. The darkness, chilled expanse
of nothing and nothing,
how it tinges your eyes with cobalt,
how daffodils careen towards it,
how hulked maples are frozen fountains,
their fingers reaching.

The Wallet

A gentle arc in leather, pocket-pressed,
curved sharply at the corners; weathered hide,
the tiny geometrics in the flesh
age-torn where seam and edge have creased. Inside:

a debit card, a Visa, MCP,
social insurance number, Blue Cross Care.
In a plastic flap, adjacent teacher ID,
he kept our faces in a family picture.

The day he drove himself along the shore
my mother, stirring in her seat, could hear
him talk of politics and not the tight

grip on his chest. And waiting for the doctor,
he didn't say a word, but turned to her
with his wallet, yellow eyes and all their weight.

Aubade

Forgive me anything, but not

how the light crawls through the window, caterpillars the walls,
    scuffs the floor to bed wheels tile by tile, climbs yellowed-grey
    bed legs screw by screw, blue bedsheets grain by grain; not
how it shines a little life on your fingers knuckle by knuckle, fills in
    the creases of skin furrow by furrow, makes blood visible vein by
    vein; not
how it milkens the strange tube strung from your arm, bleaches
    the johnny coat that clothes your body, smoothes each shaded
    crinkle on chest and shoulder; not
how it prolongs the pink of your lips, augments the soft flesh of your
    cheeks, illuminates once more the highlights in your tousled
    hair.

Forgive me anything, but not

how the lengthened hiss of breath is soothing, the hum and
    beep of monitor is salving, the feeble drumming in your chest
    unfaltering; not
how the prayers you mouthed rewind by the hour, the *amens* by the
    minute, the replay of sound by the syllable; not
how the action of your throat extends the accent in your voice, the
    aubade you must sing, yellow hammer, bird-mother, the vigour
    and camber of it.

Forgive me anything else, but not

how I want your slow pangs this last moment, the suffered echo of
    our cadence.

THE HERO COMETH

His heart seized up on a day like any other.
The sun smiled, no more, no less than usual,
no pigeons burst from perches by the multitudes,
no stores closed, and no strollers left the park
where pond water rippled as if slapping a knee.

He'd hoped a brass band would march by blowing
"The Ride of the Valkyries" through the streets.
Instead, bracing his chest through black Armani,
he slumped to earth, brow crinkled in surprise
at the irksome asphalt supporting his face.

He'd scowl if he could see the crow that skips
across the granite slab above him. Too damned
obvious with its puffed-out plume vest, crown
sleeked just so, a furl fixed above bead eyes,
and leaden beak curved in patronizing gravity.

AND YOU WERE NEVER MORE THERE

Still, slick in paved dampness,
                              a starling on its wing,
one neatly folded in snow below the body, the other
perfectly feathered,
                        frozen to her side.
Legs stretched lateral, their burnt orange
sheathed in a slush of gravel.

                        This denies
the idea of starling; she is the one you'll remember
of all the others swarming in a wing-blur.
                                        There's a certain
preservation in the way the upper beak has been
snapped off,
                        its scraps like cracked almond shells;
the way this handles your senses,
                                    wrings out experience.

You've seen nothing more beautiful.

The epigraph in "The Berry Pickers" is from Philip Larkin's poem "Nothing to Be Said."

"Some Functions of Calmia" owes its inspiration to Don McKay's "Some Functions of a Leaf."

"Field Work," "The Blacksmith," "Visitation," "From Polka to Reel," and "Triolet for a Mother" draw on a variety of the classical Homeric Hymns for their mythological precedents. "The Blacksmith" itself is written in the byr a thoddaid form, a traditional Welsh syllabic metre.

The italicized lines in "Wear It Red Against the Night" are from Alden Nowlan's poem "Canadian Love Song."

"The Hag" refers to a Newfoundland folkloric interpretation of sleep paralysis.

"Below the Spruce" is an altered form of the traditional Japanese haibun.

Both the title and beginning epigraphs of "Lords of Large Experience" come from various sections of Alfred Tennyson's "In Memoriam" stanzas.

The epigraph in "Driving the 330 from Gander" is from Lorna Crozier's poem "Winter Birches."

"Visitation" is for Andrew, "Late Poem for H." is for Heather, "Lords of Large Experience" is for Brian, "Below the Spruce" is for my father Alex, and "Kayaking on the Terra Nova River" and "Can You Ride Horses There?" are for Karen.

ACKNOWLEDGEMENTS

Earlier mouldings of some of these poems have previously appeared in *The Antigonish Review*, CV2, *The Independent*, *Iota*, *The Newfoundland Quarterly*, *Rhythm Poetry Magazine*, *The Panhandler*, *The Society 2008*, and *Zeugma*. Thank you to the editors of each of these publications.

An early version of this manuscript was a finalist for the Fresh Fish Award for Emerging Writers (2008).

"The Hag" and "Aubade" won recognition in Memorial University's Gregory J. Power Poetry Awards (2005 and 2006 respectfully).

My gratitude to the readers: Mary Dalton, Amy Evans, Angela Otto, Marlene Creates, Alison Pick, Jacob McArthur Mooney, Amanda O'Blenis, Brenda Tate, Bri and everyone at The Critical Poet.

Thanks to Michael Hiscock for the author photo.

Special appreciation to everyone at Nightwood Editions for shaping this scattering of poems into a book. And to my editor, George Murray, whose keen eye, ear and understanding of the line helped sand the rough edges and polish final versions of many of these poems.

The final word for Karen, whose endless support, love and partnership are more than I could have imagined.

Stephen Rowe's poetry has appeared in *The Antigonish Review*, *CV2*, *Iota*, *The Newfoundland Quarterly*, *The Panhandler*, *Paragon 2*, *Rhythm Poetry Magazine*, *The Society 2008* and *The Toronto Quarterly*. In 2008, he was a finalist for Newfoundland's Fresh Fish Award for Emerging Writers. He was born in Heart's Content, Newfoundland and now lives in Gander with his family. To read Stephen's blog, visit www.stephenrowe.ca.